Piano Ensembles

GW01219312

Four-part student ensembles with conductor's score and optional accompaniment

Arranged by Phillip Keveren

This collection features four student favorites from
Piano Lessons Book 4 of the *Hal Leonard Student Piano Library*

TABLE OF CONTENTS

Hal Leonard Student Piano Library Authors
Barbara Kreader • Fred Kern • Phillip Keveren • Mona Rejino

Piano Ensembles Level 4 is designed for use with the fourth book of most piano methods.

Concepts in *Piano Ensembles Level 4*:

Range

Symbols

pp, p, mp, mf, f, ♯, ♮, *ritard,*
8va, loco, D.S. al Fine, 𝄋, 𝄐

cresc. —— *dim.*

Rhythm

4/4 time signature
6/8 time signature
¢ cut time

Intervals

2nd, 3rd, 4th, 5th, 6th, 7th, 8th (octave)
melodic and harmonic

ISBN 0-7935-9217-8

HAL•LEONARD®
CORPORATION
7777 W. BLUEMOUND RD. P.O. BOX 13819 MILWAUKEE, WI 53213

Visit Hal Leonard Online at
www.halleonard.com

FOREWORD

Piano study doesn't need to be lonely any more! These ensemble versions of favorite piano pieces from the *Hal Leonard Student Piano Library* will give students the pleasure and inspiration of playing with their friends.

Each selection includes:
- A conductor's score with optional teacher accompaniment

- Four student parts:
  Parts I and II for the first piano
  Parts III and IV for the second piano

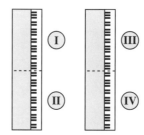

Four players at two pianos will be able to give a full and appropriate performance of each piece, yet more combinations of players and instruments are possible. Students can even add an orchestra!

Here are some ideas:
- Use four digital pianos or electronic keyboards that allow students to play the suggested instrumentation for each part.

- Double, triple, or quadruple the student parts.*

- Add the orchestral arrangement available on CD ☉ or GM disk 💾.

- Add the optional teacher accompaniment, designed for both rehearsal and performance, by using an additional piano or keyboard.

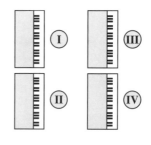

Full orchestral arrangements, available on CD #00296079 or GM disk #00296080, may be used for both performance and rehearsal:

Track 1, a **full performance version**, includes the four student parts recorded with suggested instrumentation plus an instrumental accompaniment that deepens and broadens the sound of the student ensemble.

Track 2, a **rehearsal version**, includes the four student parts recorded with suggested instrumentation and a guiding rhythm track.

If students are using a keyboard that lacks a suggested sound, other voices may be substituted. For example, if an instrument does not have "Glockenspiel," use any available similar sound, such as "Vibes" or "Marimba." If "Oboe" is unavailable, use any similar sustaining sound, such as "Flute," "Clarinet," or "Strings."

We hope you and your students will enjoy the challenges and pleasures of playing these exciting ensembles. Strike up the piano band!

Barbara Kreader   *Fred Kern*   *Phillip Keveren*   *Mona Rejino*

Due to copyright restrictions, it will be necessary to buy a new book for every four parts.

Carpet Ride
Conductor's Score & Optional Accompaniment

Performance Configurations

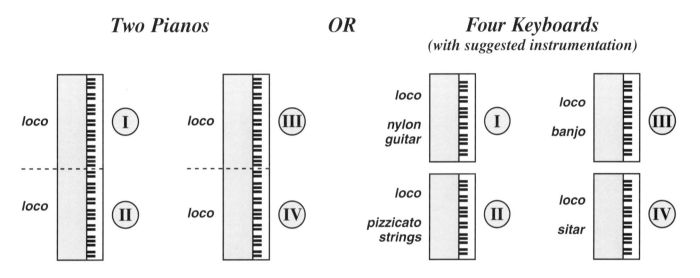

Two Pianos   OR   *Four Keyboards*
(with suggested instrumentation)

Written and arranged
by Phillip Keveren

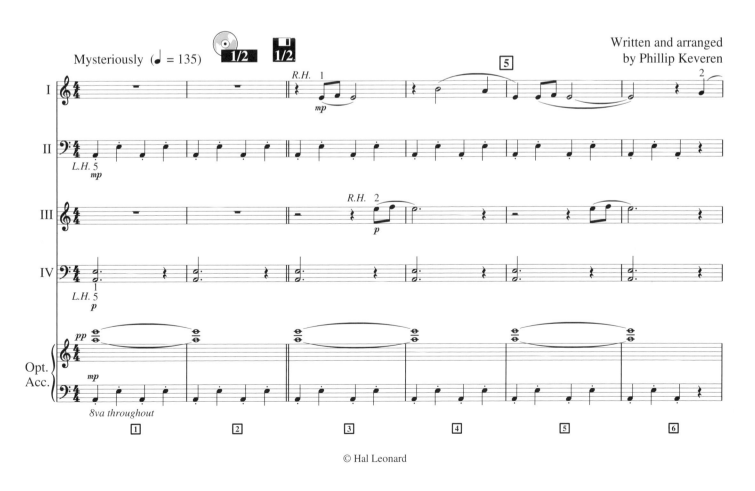

Carpet Ride – continued

Calypso Cat
Conductor's Score & Optional Accompaniment

Performance Configurations

Two Pianos

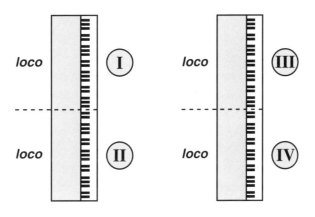

OR

Four Keyboards
(with suggested instrumentation)

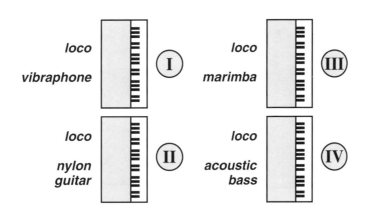

Calypso Cat

Written and arranged
by Phillip Keveren

6

If you are:
- sharing the keyboard with *Part II*, **play as written**.
- seated at your own keyboard, **play as written**.

Suggested instrumentation: **nylon guitar**

Carpet Ride

Part I

Written and arranged
by Phillip Keveren

If you are:
- sharing the keyboard with *Part II*, **play as written**.
- seated at your own keyboard, **play as written**.

Suggested instrumentation:
vibraphone

Calypso Cat
Part I

Written and arranged
by Phillip Keveren

Happily (♩ = 140)   **3/4**   **3/4**

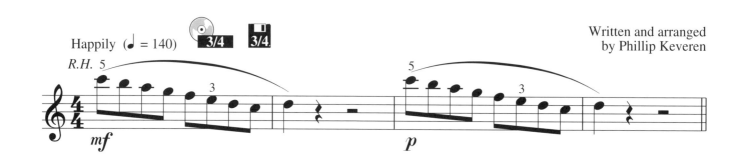

Fine

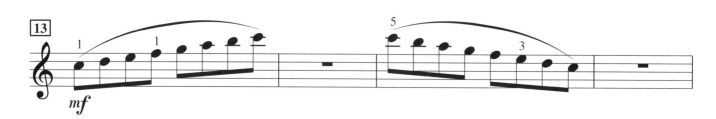

D.S. al Fine

If you are:
- sharing the keyboard with *Part I*, **play as written**.
- seated at your own keyboard, **play as written**.

Suggested instrumentation: **pizzicato strings**

Carpet Ride

Part II

Written and arranged
by Phillip Keveren

Mysteriously (♩ = 135)

DO NOT PHOTOCOPY

11

If you are:
- sharing the keyboard with *Part I*, **play as written**.
- seated at your own keyboard, **play as written**.

Suggested instrumentation:
nylon guitar

Calypso Cat

Part II

Written and arranged
by Phillip Keveren

Happily (♩ = 140) 3/4 3/4

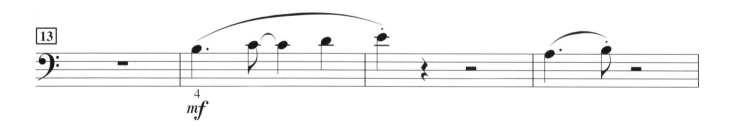

DO NOT PHOTOCOPY

If you are:
- sharing the keyboard with *Part IV*, **play as written**.
- seated at your own keyboard, **play as written**.

Suggested instrumentation: **banjo**

Carpet Ride

Part III

Written and arranged
by Phillip Keveren

If you are:
- sharing the keyboard with *Part IV*,
  play as written.
- seated at your own keyboard,
  play as written.

Suggested instrumentation:
marimba

Calypso Cat

Part III

Written and arranged
by Phillip Keveren

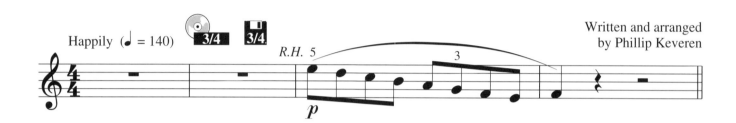

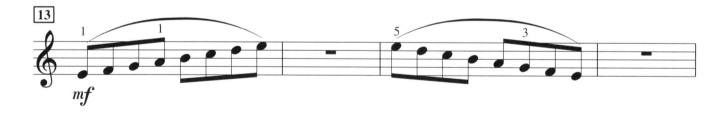

14

If you are:
• sharing the keyboard with *Part III*, **play as written**.
• seated at your own keyboard, **play as written**.

Suggested instrumentation:
sitar

Carpet Ride

Part IV

Written and arranged
by Phillip Keveren

Calypso Cat

Part IV

Written and arranged
by Phillip Keveren

Jig

Conductor's Score & Optional Accompaniment

Performance Configurations

Two Pianos

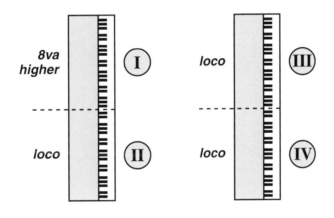

OR

Four Keyboards
(with suggested instrumentation)

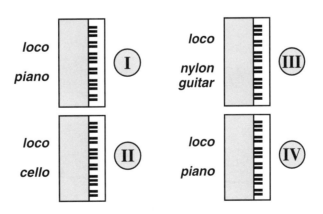

Jig

Irish
Arranged by Phillip Keveren

Irish Jig – continued

Allegro

from *Eine Kleine Nachtmusik*

Conductor's Score & Optional Accompaniment

Performance Configurations

Two Pianos *OR* *Four Keyboards*
(with suggested instrumentation)

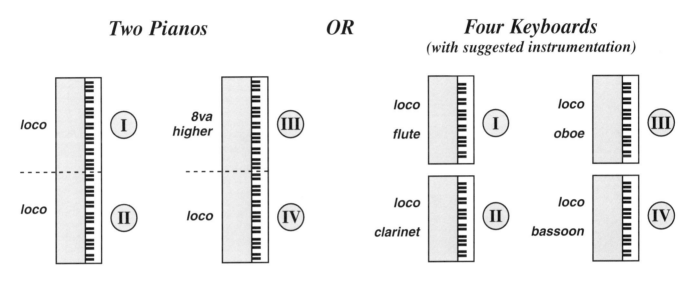

Wolfgang A. Mozart
Arranged by Phillip Keveren

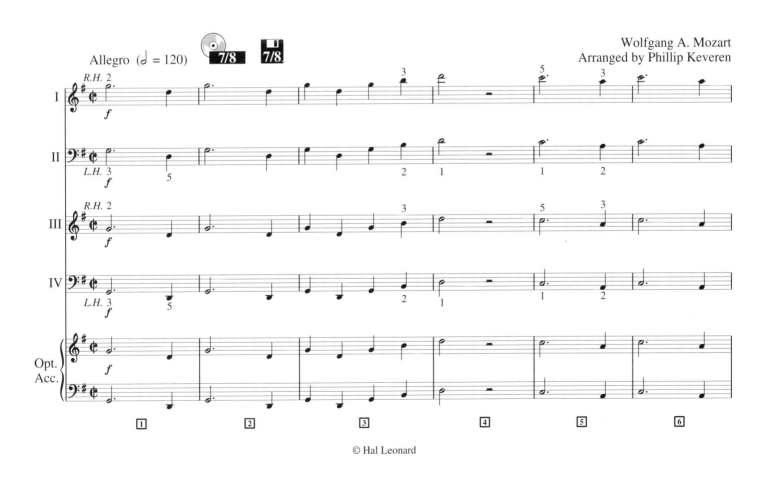

Allegro – continued

Allegro – continued

24

If you are:
• sharing the keyboard with *Part II*, **play one octave higher**.
• seated at your own keyboard, **play as written**.

Suggested instrumentation: **piano**

Jig
Part I

Irish
Arranged by Phillip Keveren

Allegro
from *Eine Kleine Nachtmusik*
Part I

Wolfgang A. Mozart
Arranged by Phillip Keveren

If you are:
- sharing the keyboard with *Part I*,
  play as written.
- seated at your own keyboard,
  play as written.

Suggested instrumentation:
cello

Jig
Part II

Irish
Arranged by Phillip Keveren

Allegro

from *Eine Kleine Nachtmusik*

Part II

Wolfgang A. Mozart
Arranged by Phillip Keveren

Jig
Part III

Irish
Arranged by Phillip Keveren

DO NOT PHOTOCOPY

If you are:
- sharing the keyboard with *Part IV*, **play one octave higher**.
- seated at your own keyboard, **play as written**.

Suggested instrumentation:
oboe

Allegro
from *Eine Kleine Nachtmusik*
Part III

Wolfgang A. Mozart
Arranged by Phillip Keveren

30

Jig
Part IV

Irish
Arranged by Phillip Keveren

If you are:
- sharing the keyboard with *Part III*, **play as written**.
- seated at your own keyboard, **play as written**.

Suggested instrumentation: **bassoon**

Allegro
from *Eine Kleine Nachtmusik*
Part IV

Wolfgang A. Mozart
Arranged by Phillip Keveren

Allegro (♩ = 120)